FUN FACTS

For
Six Year Olds

This book belongs to ....

Contents

Page 1: Amazing Animals

Page 3: Incredible Inventions

Page 5: Our Awesome Bodies

Page 7: Around the World

Page 9: Foodie Fun Facts

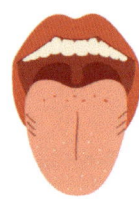

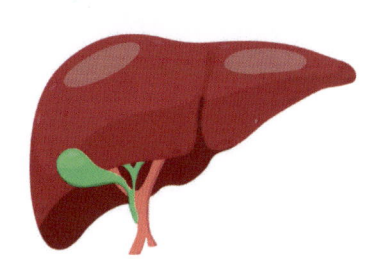

Page 11: Our Environment

Page 13: Ocean Adventures

Page 15: Super Sports

Page 17: Out of this World

Page 19: Surprising Facts

Page 21: Quiz Time

Amazing Animals

Nymph (baby mayfly)   Adult mayfly

The mayfly is the animal that lives for the shortest time as an adult. They can live as a nymph in water for up to 7 years, but once they turn into a fly, they die within 1 day.

There is a bird called a swift that spends most of its life flying. One study found that in 10 months, the swift only landed for 2 hours!

Roosters tilt their heads back to close their ears when they do their "cock-a-doodle-doo". This helps to protect their hearing like built-in earplugs!

The biggest squid ever found was bigger than a bus! It was 50 feet long. That's more than 12 six-year-olds lying in a row from head to toe!

The collective noun for porcupines is a prickle!

The howler monkey is the loudest land animal.

Axolotls can re-grow legs and other body parts if they get damaged.

One pufferfish can make enough poison (toxin) to kill 30 adult humans. There is no known cure for being poisoned by a pufferfish.

An ostrich can kick so hard that it could kill a lion!

Polar bears actually have black skin under their white fur. This helps to keep them warm by absorbing heat.

Rhino horns are made from the same thing as human hair and nails— a protein called keratin.

Orangutans are the heaviest animals that live in trees. Male orangutans weigh as much as humans!

Greenland sharks can live as long as 400 years. They live in very cold water and are rarely seen.

Rabbits are the only land mammals to have totally furry feet! They don't have pads on the bottom of their paws like dogs and cats do.

Cuckoo birds lay their eggs in other birds' nests. The other bird raises the cuckoo chicks with its own chicks.

Incredible Inventions

A 16-year-old named George Nissen invented the trampoline. He was inspired by the safety nets they used to catch circus acrobats.

Chester Greenwood invented the earmuffs when he was 15! They were originally made from beaver fur.

Louis Braille developed a way for blind people to read when he was 15. He lost his own eyesight at age 3 and created a system of raised bumps that represent letters. 200 years later, braille is still used by blind people to read.

At age 13, Ann Du created the Sign Language Glove, which translates sign language into spoken words and text.

Lego was invented by a toy maker from Denmark. Lego comes from the Danish phrase "leg godt" which means, play well!

The oldest wheel dates back over 5,000 years. Before the wheel, people could only carry things on their backs or on sledges. After the wheel, it allowed people to create carts and wagons which made it much easier to transport things.

GPS stands for Global Positioning System. This is what Google maps uses to show us where to go and track us as we go along that route. It works because there are lots of satellites around the Earth that send signals to help us see exactly where we are.

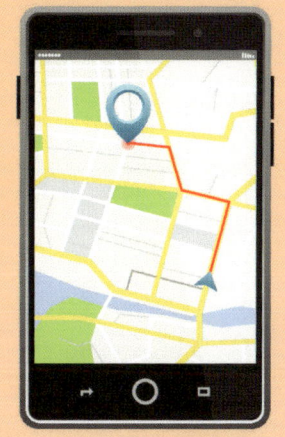

The original TV remote control was attached to the TV with a wire. It was nicknamed "lazy bones".

The pop-up toaster was invented in 1921 by a man named Charles Strite. Over 90% of people in the UK and USA have this kind of toaster.

The first electric toothbrush had to be plugged in to be used. It was designed for people who couldn't move their arms or hands well enough to brush with a manual toothbrush.

The polaroid camera was invented by an American called Edwin Land. He invented it because his daughter wanted to see the photo he had taken straight away! It took him 4 years to make, and it earned him millions of dollars over the rest of his lifetime.

The first microwave oven was nicknamed "Speedy Weenie" by its creator. He actually discovered the idea of cooking food by accident while he was working on something else. The first microwaves went on sale in 1967.

Our Awesome Bodies

Fingernails grow up to 4 times faster than toenails.

A burp is air that was accidentally swallowed while eating.

Most people know that everyone has unique fingerprints, but did you know that every person also has a different tongue print?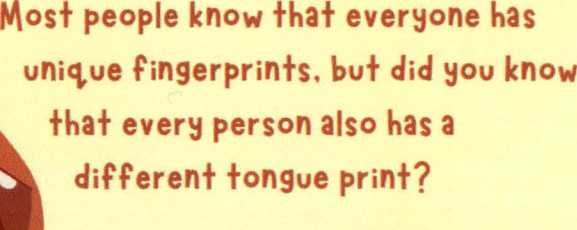

We have between 2,000 and 10,000 taste buds, and we make all new ones every 2 weeks! Taste buds are not just on the tongue. They are also on the roof of your mouth and inside your cheeks.

Your body makes enough spit in your lifetime to fill 2 swimming pools! Spit helps you taste, swallow, start digesting food and fight germs.

The largest organ is the skin. The largest organ INSIDE the body is the liver. When you are born your liver is about 5cm long. It keeps growing until you are 15.

Smiling can trick your brain into thinking you're happy even if you are feeling sad. It can also help you feel less stressed and lower your blood pressure.

1 out of every 10 people is left handed. Left-handed people tend to be more creative and more musical.

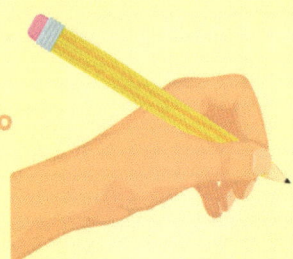

Sneezes can come out at 100 miles per hour!

Your ears can hear even when you are sleeping, but your brain chooses to ignore most sounds.

Your heart is the only muscle that doesn't get tired.

Did you know that your eyes "see" everything upside down? Your brain has to flip it the right way up.

The black part of your eye is called the pupil. It's actually a hole that lets light in.

The coloured part around the pupil is called the iris.

Both the iris and the pupil are covered by a protective clear layer called the cornea.

Red blood cells help to carry oxygen all around our bodies. There are 5 million red blood cells in 1 drop of blood.

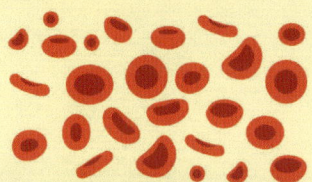

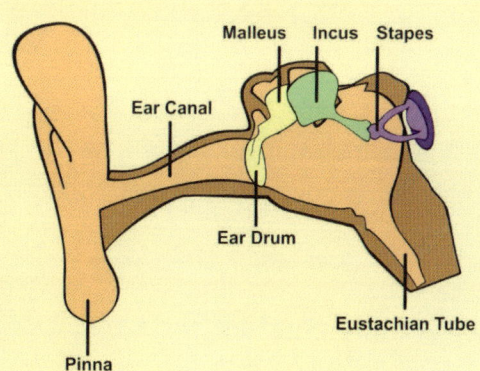

The biggest bone in your body is the femur (the thigh bone in your leg).

The smallest bone is called the stirrup (the stapes) and it's in your ear. It's only 4mm long!

Around the World

The smallest country in the world is the Vatican City. It is surrounded by Rome which is the capital of Italy.

The tallest mountain on land is called Mount Everest. The tallest mountain under the sea is called Mauna Kea, and it is actually taller than Mount Everest!

The Sahara desert is in the North of Africa. It is one of the hottest deserts in the world. It has actually snowed there three times in the last 50 years!

The Nile in Africa is the longest River in the world.

The official name for the UK is the "United Kingdom of Great Britain and Northern Ireland". This makes it the longest name for any country.

The largest country is Russia. The second largest is Canada and third largest is China.

There is a lake called the "Dead Sea" that is so salty, everyone floats in it. This means you can't sink! The saltiest sea is the Red Sea.

There are seven continents on our planet. They are:

1. Africa
2. Asia
3. Antarctica
4. Europe
5. North America
6. South America
7. Oceania (also called Australasia)

Antarctica is mostly covered by ice. Some scientists visit, but nobody lives there all the time. However, there are around 40 million penguins!

Africa is the continent with the most countries. There are 54 countries in Africa.

Asia is the largest continent.

English is spoken by people in more than 100 countries. North America has the largest number of people who speak English as their first language.

Russia is partly in Europe and partly in Asia.

There are over 7,000 different languages in the world.

The five oceans of the world are the Pacific Ocean, the Atlantic Ocean, the Indian Ocean, the Southern Ocean, and the Arctic Ocean.

Foodie Fun Facts

If you eat too many carrots, your skin can start to go orange!

Blueberries used to be called star berries because of the star-like shape on the ends.

kidney bean

Edamame bean

butter bean

broad bean

The first food eaten in space was apple sauce! The first food grown in space was the potato.

Butter beans, kidney beans, broad beans, and edamame are all poisonous when raw. They must be cooked before eating.

If you start from a seed, it takes between 3 and 6 years to grow one pineapple.

The smallest fruit in the world is called wolffia. It is the size of a grain of rice and floats on ponds.

Chili peppers taste hot because they have a chemical that makes your brain think your mouth is burning.

One cow can produce about 200,000 (two hundred thousand) glasses of milk in its lifetime!

Pumpkins are actually fruits, not vegetables. They can grow as big as a small car!

There are more than 2,000 types of cheese.

Lemon juice can kill many bacteria, so it's good for cleaning. It also has lots of vitamins, minerals, and antioxidants, so it's very good for your health too.

French fries were made in Belgium. They might be called "French fries" because French is one of the languages spoken there.

The 9th of February is National Chocolate Day, Pizza Day and Pizza Pie Day!

Lobsters used to be so common that they were fed to prisoners. They were called the "poor man's chicken." Now lobsters are rarer and often served in fancy restaurants.

There are more chickens than people in the world. There are about 8 billion people and about 26 billion chickens!

Our Environment

Here is how long it takes for different things to decompose (break down into the tiny parts they are made of):

- Vegetables: 5 days to 1 month
- Paper: 2 to 6 weeks
- Cotton t-shirts: 6 months
- Nylon fishing nets: 40 years
- Tin cans: 50 years
- Aluminium cans: 80 to 100 years
- Batteries: 100 years
- Synthetic fabric: over 100 years
- Hairspray bottles: 200 to 500 years
- Plastic: about 450 years on average, but some can take up to 10,000 years!
- Nappies (diapers): 500 years
- Car tyres: 2,000 years
- Glass: over 1 million years
- Aluminium foil: never
- Styrofoam: never

Every year, up to 14 million tons of plastic trash are dumped into the ocean.

Only about 9% of all the plastic ever made has been recycled.

About 300 million tons of plastic are made every year. Almost half of this is used just once and then thrown away.

Alternatives to plastic:
- Shampoo and conditioner bars (not bottles)
- Beeswax fabric food wraps (not clingfilm)
- Bamboo toothbrushes
- Deodorant bars
- Fabric shopping bags
- Natural sponges
- Wooden hairbrushes
- Compostable bin bags
- Bars of soap

About a quarter of the world's coral reefs have been destroyed.

Nearly 10 million trees are cut down every year just to make toilet paper.

Farming cows for meat is one of the biggest reasons trees are cut down. Cows need 28 times more space than pigs or chickens.

Americans produce 30% of the world's rubbish, even though they are only 5% of the world's people. Plastic rubbish in the ocean kills over a million sea creatures every year.

The oceans are getting warmer and sea levels are rising because of global warming. This is bad for our environment.

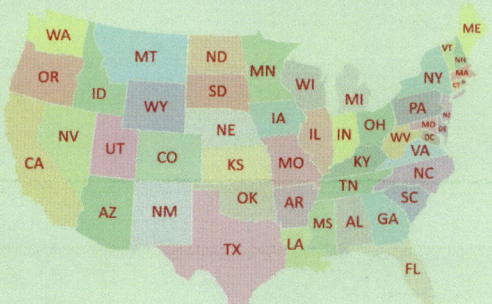

There is a giant patch of rubbish floating in the sea. It is twice the size of America! It is called the Great Pacific Garbage Patch.

Renewable energy sources are better for the environment than fossil fuels. These include:
- Solar power (from the sun)
- Wave power (from the sea)
- Hydropower (from running rivers)
- Geothermal power (from heat deep inside the Earth)
- Wind power (from wind)

Ocean Adventures

1 square inch

Octopuses have three hearts and blue blood! Some people say octopi or octopodes for more than one octopus. Actually, octopuses is the right word in English. The word octopus comes from a Greek word, so the Greek way to say more than one is octopodes. Some people think octopus comes from Latin, like the word fungus, so they say octopi, but that is not correct.

Sharks lived on Earth before trees even existed!

Turtles can breathe through their lungs or through their bottoms! They have a special way to get oxygen if they stay underwater for a long time using the blood vessels in their bottoms!

The blue whale is the biggest animal on Earth. It is actually a mammal, not a fish.

Seahorses can't swim very well. They like to hang on to coral or seaweed with their tails. Also, it is the male seahorses that get pregnant and have the babies, not the females.

Sea otters have the thickest fur of any mammal. See the square at the top of this page? A patch of otter fur that big would have between half a million and one million hairs! This helps trap a thin layer of air next to their bodies to keep them warm and helps them float.

Coral are animals! They are in the same group as jellyfish. They have to catch their own food with their tiny tentacles. Each coral is only a few millimetres long and can swim when it is very young. It then sticks to the seabed and stays there for the rest of its life.

Crabs have ten legs! The front two legs are pincers, and the other eight are for walking—sideways! Crabs have a hard protective skeleton on the outside which doesn't grow. So when the crab grows, it sheds its old shell and grows a soft new one! This can take up to a month to fully harden.

Moray eels have little shrimp "friends". The eels give food to the shrimp, and the shrimp clean the eels! Moray eels have terrible eyesight but a great sense of smell.

Moray eel

Cleaner shrimp

Killer whales are actually dolphins. They are an apex predator which means nothing hunts them. Another name for a killer whale is an orca.

Penguins (as well as some sharks and dolphins) are white on their tummies so they are hard to see from under the water and black on their backs so they blend in with the dark sea from above. This is a type of camouflage called countershading.

Super Sports

The most popular sport in the world is football (called soccer in some countries). It is played in every country in the world except for about eight countries that don't have an official team.

The word marathon is named after the Greek city of Marathon where a messenger ran about 26 miles to deliver a message about winning a battle. Today, marathons are 26.2 miles long.

Ice hockey players hit rubber discs called pucks. These used to be made of frozen cow poop!

There are cave paintings from over 9000 years ago that show early sports like swimming, wrestling, sprinting and archery.

All of the following sports were invented in Great Britain:

Rugby · Football · Cricket · Badminton · Tennis · Water polo · Rowing · Table Tennis · Squash

Ice skaters actually glide on a thin layer of water that forms as the blades on their boots melt the ice because of friction.

The average football midfielder runs about 7 miles during each match. The referees run even further than that!

Modern swimming costumes help swimmers glide through water even faster than bare skin!

The dimples in golf balls help them travel faster than if they were smooth.

In tennis, instead of saying zero, they say love.

Strange sports that are 100% real!

Cheese rolling is a sport where a huge cheese is rolled down a hill and runners race after it. The first person to cross the finish line wins the cheese!

Hot dog eating contests are a type of sport technically!

Competitive worm charming is a real sport where people try to get as many worms as possible to come out of the ground. The world record is held by Sophie Smith, who charmed 567 worms out of the ground in 2009—and she was only 10 years old at the time!

Unicycle hockey is a real sport—it's just like hockey, but played on unicycles!

Wife carrying started in Finland. Nowadays, the contestants don't actually have to be married.

Toe wrestling!

Out of this World

The Sun and the Moon look the same size in the sky because the Sun is about 400 times bigger than the Moon—but also 400 times further away!

In 2013, the Hubble Telescope spotted a blue planet that looked like Earth. However, the temperature there was over 1000°C, and it rained glass (not water!) sideways at more than 4000 miles per hour!

NASA stands for National Aeronautics and Space Administration.

A full NASA spacesuit in the 1970s cost $12 million. That would be about $150 million today. NASA's newest spacesuit is estimated to cost around $1 billion!

There are millions of pieces of space junk circling the Earth. Even tiny pieces can cause big problems if they crash into satellites.

Astronauts grow taller in space because there is less gravity acting on their bodies. Only 24 people have ever travelled into space past Earth's orbit.

Our moon

There is a theory that the Moon used to be part of the Earth. A long time ago, when Earth was a young planet, it may have been hit by something big—and a chunk broke off. That chunk became the Moon!

Mercury

Mercury and Venus are the closest planets to the sun. They are the only planets with no moons. This is because the sun's gravity is so strong that it pulls anything smaller than these planets towards itself.

Venus

Jupiter

Jupiter is made mostly of hydrogen and helium, the same elements as the Sun. If it were 80 times bigger, it could make its own energy and would be a star! Jupiter also has a Great Red Spot—a giant storm that has been going for over 100 years.

When you look at stars, you are actually seeing the past. Light from the nearest star (not counting our Sun) takes just over 4 years to reach Earth. So when you see it, you're looking at light that left that star more than 4 years ago!

If two pieces of metal touch each other in space, they will stick together forever. This is called cold welding. It happens because there is no air or water between them.

Surprising Facts

There used to be a job called a "knocker-upper". These people would be paid to knock on peoples' window and wake them up. This was before we had alarm clocks.

Did you know painting and sculpture used to be Olympic events? Medals were also given out for music and architecture.

The world's oldest living tree is in California. As of 2025, it is around 4,855 years old—older than the pyramids!

Marie Curie was the first person to win two Nobel Prizes. She received one in physics and one in chemistry. The Nobel Prize is one of the most important awards in the world. It is given to people who have done something that greatly helps humankind.

Some cats are allergic to humans!

Just like Earth has earthquakes, the Moon shakes too—they're called moonquakes!

Koalas have fingerprints almost exactly like ours. In fact, their fingerprints are so similar to human ones that even scientists need special tools to tell them apart.

A single bolt of lightning has enough energy to toast 100,000 slices of bread! That's a lot of toast from just one lightning strike.

Umbrellas were first invented to protect people from the sun. They were only later used for rain.

The first computer was as big as a whole room.

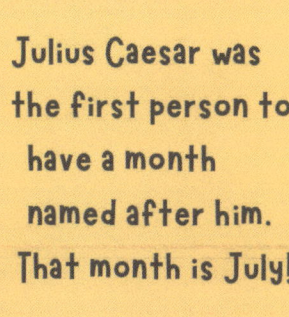

Julius Caesar was the first person to have a month named after him. That month is July!

The Great Wall of China is 20,000 km long and took 2,000 years to build! People used to think you could see it from space, but actually it is not wide enough to see without help.

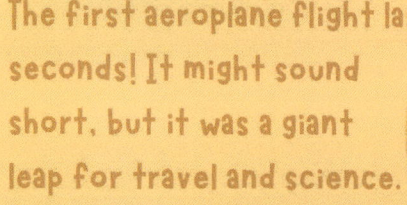

The first aeroplane flight lasted only 12 seconds! It might sound short, but it was a giant leap for travel and science.

Golf is the only sport that has ever been played on the Moon! An astronaut hit a golf ball up there in 1971!

Earthworms don't have a heart like humans do, but they have five special organs that pump blood around their bodies. So you could say they have five hearts!

QUIZ TIME

Test yourself and see what you can remember.
You can find all of the answers in this book!

1. What were umbrellas originally used for?

2. Do astronauts get taller or shorter in space?

3. What were ice hockey pucks originally made of?

4. Which animal has the thickest fur?

5. What happens if you eat too many carrots?

6. Which animal has fingerprints very similar to humans?

7. Name two really weird sports.

8. What came first, sharks or trees?

9. Who invented a way for blind people to read using raised dots?

10. What is one reason we cut down trees?

11. Where were French fries developed?

12. Name an old-fashioned Olympic event.

13. How long did the first aeroplane flight last?

14. When you look at the stars, how far into the past are you looking?

15. Name three sports invented in Great Britain.

16. What were blueberries originally called?

17. How many different languages are there in the world?

18. Name the smallest fruit in the world.

19. Name a renewable energy source.

20. What is a knocker-upper?

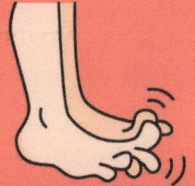

More books by Stephanie Lipsey-Liu

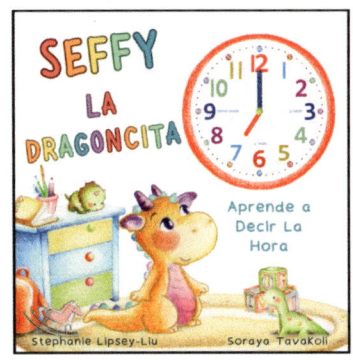 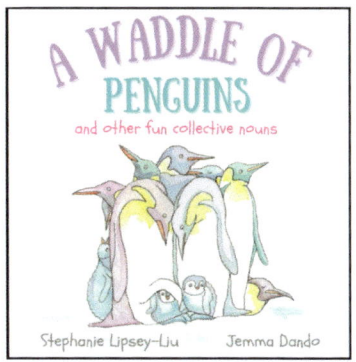 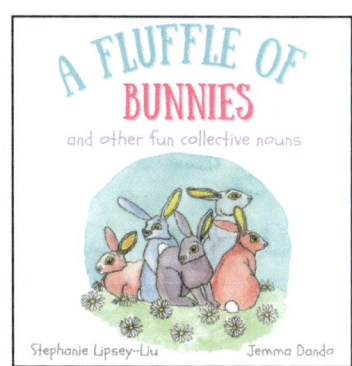
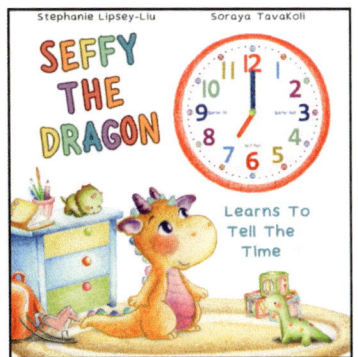  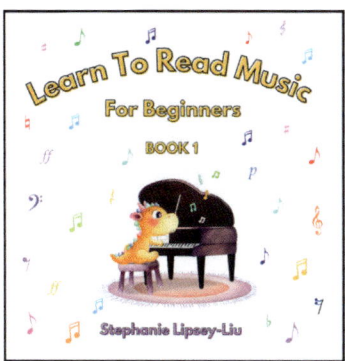

This book is Copyright © 2024 by Stephanie Lipsey-Liu.
All rights reserved

No part of this publication may be reproduced or transmitted in any form or by any means, electronic or mechanical, including photocopying, recording, scanning or otherwise, or through any information browsing, storage or retrieval system, without permission in writing from the publisher.

First printed 2024 ISBN 978-1-917565-03-5

Little Lion Publishing UK

Nottingham, England

www.littlelionpublishing.co.uk

Printed in Dunstable, United Kingdom